George Cruikshank's

The Worship of Bacchus in focus

Robert Upstone

With a technical essay by Christopher Holden

TATE PUBLISHING

Displays from the Collection, sponsored by BP

Front cover: George Cruikshank,
The Worship of Bacchus 1860–2 (detail)

Back cover: *The Worship of Bacchus* 1860–2
(detail, fig.14)

Frontispiece: *The Worship of Bacchus* 1860–2
(detail)

Published by order of the Tate Trustees 2001
on the occasion of the exhibition at Tate Britain,
23 May – 2 December 2001

ISBN 1 85437 405 2

A catalogue record for this publication is
available from the British Library

Published by Tate Publishing, a division of
Tate Enterprises Ltd, Millbank, London SW1P 4RG

Designed and typeset by Caroline Johnston

Measurements are given in centimetres,
height before width

Printed and bound in Great Britain by
Balding + Mansell, Norwich

Published with the support of the
Paul Mellon Centre for Studies in British Art

George Cruikshank's
The Worship of Bacchus in focus

Contents

Foreword

The Worship of Bacchus (1860–2) by George Cruikshank (1792–1878), a visual essay on the social evils of alcohol, is an eccentric masterpiece of Victorian art which has not been displayed for nearly a century. Presented to the National Gallery in 1869 after a public subscription organised by the artist and his colleagues in the Temperance movement, this vast and astonishing picture was passed in quick succession from the South Kensington Museum to Bradford Art Gallery, to Dundee Art Gallery and finally to the Temperance Memorial Hall, Newcastle, where it remained until 1909. In 1959 it was transferred by the National Gallery to the Tate Gallery, where it was kept in store until, following the launch of Tate Britain last year, a major restoration project was begun by Tate conservator Christopher Holden in readiness for our 2001 displays.

As an impassioned and ambitious work both conceptually and visually, *The Worship of Bacchus* is richly revealing about its maker and its era. As such it plays a distinctive part in this year's various events exploring aspects of nineteenth-century Britain in recognition of the centenary of Queen Victoria's death, and it forms a fascinating subject for the second in Tate Britain's new series of small in-focus displays, which began last year with *William Hogarth's Sigismunda*. This series, whose catalogues are kindly supported by the Paul Mellon Centre for Studies in British Art, forms part of Tate Britain's Displays from the Collection, sponsored by BP.

The display is also an eloquent advertisement for the skills of Tate's conservation team in general and Christopher Holden's work in particular. The transformation of the picture from its severely degraded state a year ago has been a truly remarkable process, a difficult journey keenly supported by many people, not least John Anderson and his team who have made a magnificent new frame. Above all we must salute Tate Curator Robert Upstone, who proposed the display, wrote the majority of this catalogue, has been a persuasive advocate of the work's significance and potential, and who worked tirelessly and efficiently on the project alongside Tate Britain Curator Martin Myrone. From beyond Tate, William Feaver, who campaigned long ago for the picture's restoration, has been consistently helpful, and Andrew Graham-Dixon responded immediately and brilliantly to our suggestion that he should make and present a television film about the work: *1000 ways of getting drunk in England* (BBC, 2001) is the result – a perfect complement to the present exhibition. Thanks are also due to our lenders, especially the V&A and Stella Beddoe of the Brighton Museum; Jan Piggott, Sarah Hyde, Nicola Bion, Brian Allen and Patrick McCaughey.

Stephen Deuchar
Director, Tate Britain

The Demon Drink

Robert Upstone

> To omit the name of George Cruikshank from the history of England
> in the nineteenth century would be to leave out an essential factor
> from the story of the passions, merriments and moods of the people.
>
> (*Publisher's Circular*, 16 February 1878)[1]

Preferences
Hero	Nelson, Wellington
Artist	Raphael, – or myself. Hogarth
Virtue	Honesty, Honest charity
Occupation	Drawing and painting to prevent evil and try to do good
Motto	At it again. Nil desperandum. Vis fortibus arma.
Dislike	Humbug. Alcohol

(from a list of 'Preferences' made by Cruikshank *c*.1866)[2]

The publisher's statement above was made the year he died, but George
Cruikshank is regularly omitted from accounts of British art, and his
greatest work has lain unseen for nearly a century, waiting to be brought
back to life. Without doubt one of the most original, ambitious and didac-
tic works in British painting, his vast canvas *The Worship of Bacchus*
(1860–2) has not been displayed since 1909. It is an encyclopaedic inven-
tory of the Victorian relationship with alcohol, intended to sum up all
Cruikshank's passionately held beliefs about the social damage of drink,
and to alert and convert all who saw it. It was presented to the nation by
subscribers in 1869.

Teeming with figures, *The Worship of Bacchus* (fig.1) illustrates meticu-
lously all the evils and horrors of alcohol – a zealous, animated manifesto
rather than just a work of art. Every section of nineteenth-century British
society is included, every element of the state, and it also shows alcohol
being foisted on previously teetotal cultures of the new Empire. The
painting is a dense network of vignettes, presided over by the statue of
Bacchus, the Roman God of wine and drunken revelry. Ranged along the
bottom of the composition are mild, apparently innocuous scenes where
alcohol is used: a christening; a marriage feast; a birthday; and also,
tellingly, a funeral. Elsewhere judges and judiciary quaff merrily, as do
the Army and Navy, and there are scenes of bitter irony such as the boozy
charity 'Fete Champetre to aid those by gin and beer made destitute and
homeless'. At Bacchus's foot, brewers and distillers dispense drink to the
crowds, who, losing control, riot madly. In the immensely complex tangle
of figures men and women punch, kick, claw and kill; policemen struggle
to gain control, but even some of them are drunk. A man with side-
whiskers, resembling young Cruikshank, strikes out at his wife (fig.2). A
lunatic, broken free of his straight-jacket, dances wildly on a tomb that

fig.2 *The Worship of Bacchus* (detail)

Cruikshank has inscribed: 'Sacrificed at the shrine of Bacchus father, mother, sister, brother, wife, children, property, friends, body and mind.' Beneath this a widow looks out blankly at us, surrounded by children in poverty bearing placards reading 'No father, no mother'. At the top of the picture lie the harshest consequences. Men are flogged; a ship, on fire through negligence, heads for the rocks; a train has crashed; a man is led to the gibbet to be hanged for a drink-fuelled murder. Ranged along the horizon are all the institutions to which alcohol provides inmates: the ragged school, workhouse, prison, asylum, magdalen hospital for prostitutes, and the cemetery. Cruikshank aptly subtitled his picture 'The Drinking Customs of Society, from the Cradle to the Grave'. It is difficult to sum up adequately all that is happening, and Cruikshank himself published a lecture about it, selections from which are reproduced on page 30.

Principally an illustrator, Cruikshank made relatively few oils, and *Bacchus* is not a particularly painterly picture. However, the enormously detailed, complex design, is a superb piece of composition, which shows off his skills of draughtsmanship. Astonishing in its hyperbole, the picture is unrelenting in hammering home its message. It offers a unique vision of the world from which it comes, its manners, morals, vices and hypocrisies, and the ideals of those who sought to change them. But it

also bears testimony to the inventiveness and beliefs of George Cruikshank, a remarkable figure usually left out of histories of British art,
whose own commitment to teetotalism, while fiercely passionate, was
rarely sanctimonious, and usually humane and grounded in pragmatism.
With present-day concerns about what Home Secretary Jack Straw
described in autumn 2000 as our own 'drunken yob' culture - about the
damage to health caused by alcohol, and its relationship to crime and
social corrosion, and the debate around the relaxation of drug laws -
Cruikshank's masterpiece may perhaps hold resonance and relevance for
a contemporary audience. Indeed, Cruikshank's vision of an urban, indus-
trialised Victorian society falling apart and desperately searching for
meaning, is a very modern one. If Cruikshank is wrong to exaggerate
alcohol use and abuse to the status of a cause, rather than merely as a
symptom of social strife, his characterisation of alienation rings dis-
turbingly true.

Images of the pleasures and pitfalls of the bottle are found in British
art as far back as Hogarth's morality series such as *Industry and Idleness*,

fig.3 *The Worship of Bacchus*
(detail)

fig.4 William Hogarth
(1697–1764)
Gin Lane 1751
Engraving 35.7 × 30.5 cm
Tate

Gin Lane (fig.4) and *Beer Street*, and *The Rake's Progress*. But with the advent of Victorian moralism, the seemliness of such hard-hitting material as subjects for fine art was put in doubt, and they were rarely imitated. Cruikshank's *Bacchus* is one of the few paintings of the Victorian era to try to engage seriously with the subject of drink head-on. Hogarth was not greatly admired in the second half of the century because of his ribald excess, although typically he was much admired by Cruikshank. The bitter furore caused by the exhibition in London in 1894 of Degas's *L'absinthe* vividly illustrates continued sensitivity to images of the effects of drink, even in the 'naughty nineties'. It has been left until recent decades for the causes and effects of excessive drinking to be investigated in British art again in works such as Gilbert and George's *Balls: The Evening Before the Morning After* and *Gordons Makes us Drunk* (both 1972), and recent videos of alcoholics by Gillian Wearing. These too, however, remain rare examples.

George Cruikshank

George Cruikshank (1792–1878) was one of the most prolific and famous illustrators of the nineteenth century, his long career stretching from the Napoleonic Wars, when his father taught him etching, to the time he died in 1878. His early works were biting political satires of Bonaparte and the British Government, with the Prince Regent (later George IV) a prime tar-

fig.1 George Cruikshank
The Worship of Bacchus 1860–2
Oil on canvas 236 × 406
Tate

get. Cruikshank showed him as a porcine, wine-guzzling buffoon, a moron ruled by infantile passions and goatish lust. Cruikshank's 1819 caricature of the Regent breaking wind in Parliament's face surely ranks as one of the most deliberately offensive and provocative images ever produced. The following year the Crown paid Cruikshank, along with other caricaturists, the enormous sum of £100 to stop showing George in an unpleasant light. But Cruikshank was soon back at it, and it was these early political images, so subversive and humorous, but with an implicit popular morality and sense of justice, that brought him long-lasting fame.

With the passing of Georgian England, and the calming of British politics, Cruikshank turned to illustrating books and producing enormously inventive social satires. Book markets were growing and publishing boomed. His immensely popular illustrations to fairy stories Ruskin believed the equal of Rembrandt's etchings, and further celebrity came from his annual *Comic Almanac*, and his famous plates to Charles Dickens's *Sketches by Boz* and *Oliver Twist*. Cruikshank worked prodigiously and hard, to an exacting standard, and it is estimated he completed 10,000 designs in his lifetime.

But in 1847, at the age of fifty-five, Cruikshank turned to temperance, and while he never lost his sharp sense of humour, the remaining thirty years of his life were devoted to bringing social reform through teetotalism. His father Isaac had drunk himself to death in April 1811, when Cruikshank was nineteen, downing a bottle of spirits in a drinking competition that put him into a coma from which he never regained consciousness. George drank hard and often in his youth and well into

fig.5 George and Eliza
Cruikshank c.1862
Photograph
Victoria & Albert Museum,
London

fig.6 George Cruikshank
Comic Almanac: Wine in a
Ferment and Spirits in Hot
Water 1844
Etching
Dr Jan Piggott

Wine in a Ferment and Spirits in Hot Water.

middle age. He and his brother Robert racketted around London low-life in the period immediately after their father's death, and George continued the pattern, sometimes going missing from home for days, and still going on alcoholic marathons with his friends in his thirties and forties. He enjoyed the bonhomie of the tavern, smoked endless pipes and sang comical songs, his friend W.H. Wills writing that in this period 'surely no man drank with more fervour and enjoyment, nor carried his liquor so kindly, so merrily'.[3] But increasingly he came to perceive the intemperate use of alcohol as an evil. He included *The Gin Juggernaut* in his 1835 *Sketch Book*, a plate depicting a horrifying mobile gin palace which crushes all before it, bringing darkness and misery. His 1844 *Comic Almanac* plate 'Wine in a Ferment and Spirits in Hot Water' (fig.6) is a humorous riposte to temperance, as well as evidence of Cruikshank's extraordinary imagination. His portrayal of *A Gin Shop* for *Sketches by Boz* (1836) was a piece of realism, showing a fight breaking out in the background, a cad trying to seduce the barmaid, a child waiting for alcohol and a man on crutches, literally on his last legs, waiting at the bar for his next gin fix. These were all motifs that later found more extreme expression in *The Worship of Bacchus*. Dickens himself considered gin shops inevitable attractions if the social conditions of the poor were not raised, but not, he wrote in *Sketches by Boz*, the cause of such misery in themselves – a position that later alienated the old friends from each other. But Dickens's account in his essay of the fight near closing time has echoes of the riot in Cruikshank's *Bacchus*. A knot of arguing labourers, Dickens wrote,

> finding it impossible to silence one man, who is particularly anxious
> to adjust the difference, they resort to the expedient of knocking
> him down and jumping on him afterwards ... a scene of riot and

confusion ensues ... the landlord hits everybody, and everybody hits the landlord; the barmaids scream; the police come in; the rest is a confused mixture of arms, legs, staves, torn coats, shouting, and struggling. Some of the party are borne off to the station-house, and the remainder slink home to beat their wives for complaining, and kick the children for daring to be hungry.[4]

Like Cruikshank, Dickens was a keen investigator of London low-life, and this account was intended to have the ring of recognisable reality.

The Bottle

The turning-point in Cruikshank's life and career came with his decision to undertake *The Bottle*. Like a Zola novel, in a series of eight prints Cruikshank outlined the progressive decline of a once prosperous, flourishing mechanic and his family through unemployment, impoverishment, begging, child death, domestic violence, murder and eventual insanity (figs.7, 8). It is a shocking sequence of compositionally taut designs, unflinching in their realism. That Cruikshank made them demonstrates he was already flirting with temperance. His friend Wills remembered him around 1846 declining an invitation to a supper party lest he should be tempted to drink, but turning up later, imbibing excessively, and ending up climbing a lamp-post in the street outside.[5] Cruikshank evidently struggled to moderate his drinking, but it was when he showed *The Bottle* to William Cash, Chairman of the National Temperance Society, that his real crisis of conscience came. Cash challenged him simply why, if he was so aware of the bottle's harm, he was not a teetotaler? Cruikshank was 'completely staggered' in his own words. Unable to give any adequate explanation to Cash or himself, he resolved 'to give his example as well as his art to the total abstainers'.[6]

The prints caused a sensation, and sold 100,000 copies in just a few weeks. There were deluxe editions, which actually sold poorly, but Cruikshank also produced a shilling set, and later a sixpenny one, so that low-income families might afford them. His friend Henry Mayhew, interviewing an 'intelligent costermonger' for his survey of *London Labour and the London Poor* (1851), was told Cruikshank's 'Bottle was much admired' among the poor, although he reported a man who said it 'showed what "lush" did' being seen again blind drunk three hours later.[7] Bottle mania swept the country; pirated prints soon appeared; the designs were used on tea services (fig.9), tapping the rise of temperance-led tea drinking; there were theatrical dramatisations and wax tableaux; and Mathew Arnold and several lesser poets were moved to pen unfortunate verses. The prints were also admired on the Continent. Cruikshank immediately produced a sequel, *The Drunkard's Children* (1848) (fig.10). The son and daughter, scarred by their family's collapse, become respectively a criminal and a prostitute. Caught and convicted, the youth dies in a prison hulk, while in the last plate, 'The poor girl, homeless, friendless,

THE BOTTLE. Plate I.

THE BOTTLE IS BROUGHT OUT FOR THE FIRST TIME: THE HUSBAND INDUCES HIS WIFE "JUST TO TAKE A DROP."

fig.7 George Cruikshank
The Bottle, Plate 1: The Bottle is
brought Out. For the First Time
the Husband Induces his Wife
'Just to take a Drop' 1847
Glyphograph 22 × 33
Victoria & Albert Museum,
London

THE BOTTLE. Plate III.

AN EXECUTION SWEEPS OFF THE GREATER PART OF THEIR FURNITURE: THEY COMFORT THEMSELVES WITH THE BOTTLE.

fig.8 George Cruikshank
The Bottle, Plate 3: An Execution
Sweeps off the Greater Part of
their Furniture. They comfort
themselves with the Bottle 1847
Glyphograph 22 × 33
Victoria & Albert Museum,
London

deserted, destitute, and gin mad, commits self murder,' throwing herself off Waterloo Bridge, infamous for prostitution. Around five hundred Victorian women drowned themselves in the Thames each year, often in the same circumstances as the drunkard's daughter.[8] She reappears in *The Worship of Bacchus*, on the left in a green dress, hurling herself into the fray below (fig.11). Motifs from the two series are quoted by artists as diverse as Charles Allston Collins, George Frederic Watts, Gustave Doré, Paul Gavarni and Augustus Leopold Egg. Robert Braithwaite Martineau's

fig.9 Temperance Tea Plate
Illustrated with *The Bottle*
*c.*1847
Earthenware 22 × 22
Brighton and Hove Museums

fig.10 George Cruikshank
The Drunkard's Children, Plate 1:
The Gin Shop 1848
Glyphograph 22 × 33
Victoria & Albert Museum,
London

fig.11 *The Worship of Bacchus*
(detail)

fig.12 Robert Braithwaite
Martineau (1826–69)
The Last Day in the Old Home
1862
Oil on canvas 107.3 × 144.8
Tate

morality tale *The Last Day in the Old Home* (1862; fig.12) seems partly inspired by the bailiff scene in *The Bottle*. Painted the same year as *Bacchus*, drink is only a part of its narrative, but the young boy's introduction to champagne, and likely repetition of his father's profligacy, mirror Cruikshank's concerns.

Demon Drink – The Context

Following his conversion, Cruikshank lectured tirelessly on temperance, an admired, theatrical, highly effective speaker. When the celebrated John Gough visited from America to speak for the cause, Cruikshank introduced him at the gathering in Sadler's Wells Theatre. So many people surged forward to sign the pledge that Cruikshank swiftly placed a plank over the orchestra pit and assisted them onto the stage, an incident he commemorated in a plate for the *Illustrated London News* and also in Gough's autobiography. Temperance was a mass movement, in Cruikshank's day a following of around three million people being claimed (out of a total population of about 20 million)[9]. It was far from being the extremist, minority, quirky movement of our popular imagination. The physical dangers of drink had become known through medical discovery, and evidence of the social destruction alcohol caused was readily visible in the Victorian city. Cheap beer and spirits were available in pubs and gin palaces literally on every corner, and these were the venue not just for intoxication but for every social activity. Urban water supplies were horribly polluted, in London drawn from the same River Thames which received the capital's sewage. Beer was a safer alternative, but inevitably led to drunkenness, and attendant social problems. The teetotalers tried to sell the virtues of tea drinking, itself safer than plain water because it was boiled, and they organised attractive social activities to shift the focus of entertainment away from the pub.

But temperance was also an expression of social regulation, both behavioural and consumerist. Tea and coffee importers, inextricably linked to colonial expansion, saw opportunities to promote their trade. Industrialists wanted a sober workforce to maximise production. A sober populace too could spend their money not on drink, but on the ever-increasing range of manufactured goods. Nevertheless, the temperance movement was reformist and idealist. Writing for the Royal Commission for the Contagious Diseases Act, a law controlling prostitution, Josephine Butler described the temperance men of 1872 as 'abstainers, steady men, and to a great number members of chapels and churches, and many of them are men who have been engaged in the anti-slavery movement and abolition of the corn law movement. They are the leaders of good social movements, men who have had to do with political reforms in time past.'[10] The founders of temperance had connections to Chartism, and much of that reformatory, democratising zeal was brought to the new movement. Those involved in temperance were generally of the middle and respectable working, artisanal class; the aristocracy were not adher-

fig.13 *The Worship of Bacchus*
(detail)

ents, nor were the very poorest, whose destructive drinking the movement aimed to quell. Its power base were sober tradesman and profes-
sionals, usually Nonconformists rather than Anglicans, self-made people
for whom the idea of social progression and improvement were realities.
It was an era with an overwhelming belief in personal responsibility for
self-improvement and social circumstance. Samuel Smiles's enormously
influential book *Self Help* appeared in 1859, subtitled 'Illustrations of
Character, Conduct and Perseverance'. 'National progress,' Smiles assert-
ed, 'is the sum of individual industry, energy, and uprightness, as national
decay is of individual idleness, selfishness, and vice. What we are accus-
tomed to decry as great social evils, will ... be found to be but the out-
growth of man's own perverted life ... the highest patriotism and
philanthropy consist ... in helping and stimulating men to elevate and
improve themselves.'[11]

The temperance movement, however, were a generally compassionate
group, not usually targeting drinkers for anger but instead the distillers
and politicians who benefited from the poor's weakness. Cruikshank was
passionate in his advocacy. His biographer Jerrold recalled: 'He sometimes offended people by his denunciation of even the most moderate

drinkers, but he never made an enemy by his gaucherie or his downright phrases imported into quiet circles, because the purity of his motive and the well-known impetuosity of his nature excused him.'[12] Nevertheless, his antics were legendary:

> When dining at the Mansion House, Cruikshank, at the passing of the loving cup, would go through an extraordinary pantomime before all the company, expressive of his horror of strong drinks. He would shake his hand angrily at the Lord Mayor, and raise his hands with horror while his neighbour quaffed ... The company humoured the eccentric old gentleman; for, in their hearts, they could not but respect his downright earnestness.[13]

From his temperance talks Cruikshank seems to have been particularly interested in connections between alcohol and crime, something that underpins many of the incidents in *The Worship of Bacchus*. Speaking in 1864 he noted,

> There are a number of besettling sins connected with drinking, such as robberies, brutal assaults, garottings, house-breaking, suicide, and murder ... if we could do away with intoxicating licquors altogether, we might wheel out that dreadful instrument the gibbet ... and make a bonfire of it ... there is hardly a murder committed ... but drink has something to do with it. Remove the drink, and you will stop murder ... We should stop, if not all crimes, if not all offences, still the great majority of them; and that is what we are aiming at.[14]

Cruikshank's linking of alcohol to crime is confirmed by recent Home Office reports, which estimate that '78 per cent of assaults and 88 per cent of criminal damage cases are committed while the offender is under the influence of alcohol. Alcohol is often consumed by offenders and victims prior to the offence being committed, and it is inextricably linked to disorder.'[15] Similarly, as Cruikshank claimed, alcohol still often plays a part in unlawful killings, and the charity Alcohol Concern estimate that 60–70 per cent of men who assault their partners are drunk, and drink is associated with 65 per cent of suicide attempts.[16] Cruikshank's descriptions seem based on a continuing truth.

The Worship of Bacchus

The story of Cruikshank's *Bacchus* is nearly as complicated as its elaborate composition. The idea, he claimed, came to him in a flash in 1859, and he secured the support of a committee of influential temperance leaders to support him with 'spending money' while he undertook his great project. First Cruikshank was to make a large watercolour, which would be published as a print. This would reimburse the Committee, and pay for Cruikshank to make a large version in oils, to be exhibited and toured, which, the artist suggested, would bring even greater returns as well as enormous propaganda for the cause. Such financial reassurances should

fig.14 *The Worship of Bacchus* (detail)

fig.15 George Cruikshank
First Sketch for *The Worship of Bacchus* c.1859
Pencil and watercolour
38 × 46.5
Victoria & Albert Museum, London

have been treated cautiously, as Cruikshank was notoriously bad at estimating or controlling financial remuneration for his work.

Critics, journalists and temperance leaders visited Cruikshank's Mornington Place studio in July 1860 to see the finished watercolour, virtually identical to the subsequent oil version. Publicising the watercolour was intended to encourage subscriptions for the print. Cruikshank considered the viewings a huge success: 'Every one who has seen it declares it to be the best thing I have ever done – Frith was much taken with it – and sent his wife and children to look at it – This is very complimentary is it not?'[17] Buoyed by such reactions, Cruikshank engaged Charles Mottram to begin engraving the plate in September 1860, doing the outlines himself and Mottram filling in the detail.

But disaster soon struck. In November 1860 John Stewart, an art critic and member of the Bacchus committee, visited Cruikshank's studio. Cruikshank's notes suggest Stewart was instructed by the Committee to ask him to begin the large oil even though the engraving was far from finished. But Blanchard Jerrold provides a more convincing account that Stewart found Cruikshank already at work on the oil, saying it was 'a rest' from etching, which no man could do continuously.[18] The truth was that Cruikshank itched to get going on the great design, and the committee allowed him to continue. Cruikshank became ever more engrossed in the painting, and neglected the print. It was a fatal error. Print subscriptions were already slow, and lengthening the time taken to complete it put the project in financial jeopardy, as the engraving would be the chief source of reimbursement. It did not finally appear until 1864.

Labouring on his vast canvas, Cruikshank's spirits began to flag, and he expressed doubts to his friend William Henry Merle about whether the picture actually worked and if it was the equal of Frith's *Derby Day*, a panoramic, anthropological survey of Victorian Society at the races. Merle wrote to him not altogether comfortingly: 'your "Leviathan" ... in design & magnitude beats the "Derby Day" ... you must not expect the educated & higher order to admire your picture ... [they] know & feel that with them the *beginning* wd. not lead to *the end* as pictured above ...Your admirers, your success, will be with a humbler class.'[19] Not a teetotaller, Merle is unlikely to have reassured Cruikshank, whose pictorial agenda wavers somewhat if the premise of progressive degradation and degeneration is rejected. Frith's *Derby Day* was shown in 1858 to huge crowds, and Cruikshank clearly saw himself in competition.

The finished oil was exhibited in a small gallery next to the Lyceum Theatre in Wellington Street, five hundred people attending the private view on Monday 4 August 1862. Press reactions were highly favourable, and Cruikshank expected success. But nobody came. Jerrold recalled

> seeing him in his exhibition room. It was empty. There was a wild, anxious look in his face, when he greeted me. While we talked, he glanced once or twice at the door, when he heard any sound in that direction. Were they coming at last, the tardy, laggard public for whom he had been bravely toiling so many years. Here was his

fig.16 George Cruikshank
The Fruits of Intemperance
c.1860
Engraving 37.9 × 56
British Museum

mighty labour against the wall, and all the world had been told that it was there. His trusty friend Thackeray had hailed it in the *Times* … It was near noon, and only a solitary visitor had wandered into the room. Thackeray might well say, "How little do we think of the extraordinary powers of this man, and how ungrateful we are to him!"[20]

A move to Exeter Hall and the addition of a survey of 1,100 of Cruikshank's designs failed to remedy the situation. Trying to identify just why Cruikshank seemed no longer popular, Francis Turner Palgrave perceptively judged it was not simply differences between Georgian and Victorian taste, but because Cruikshank's parody of the dominant classes in his early works, and his continuing satire, made him unpopular in the rarefied drawing room, because 'his high tragic power has been exercised mainly against those abuses by which the poor and the helpless suffer. His sympathies are clearly those of a man of the people for the people; and this excludes drawing room popularity.'[21] More simply, *Bacchus* was probably too moralistic and fervent for even Victorian taste to stomach. It certainly provoked an adverse response in Frith's daughter Jane. 'We were commanded,' she recalled, 'to see his dreadful work. Papa was the most abstemious of men, and we are one and all teetotallers, not from any matter of principle, but simply because we do not like wine; and it was a double insult to be made to listen to the rabid abstainer while he described bit by bit the hideous picture he had spent years painting.'[22]

A tour of *Bacchus* through England, Scotland, Ireland and Wales failed to bring financial return. In Birmingham 2,000 people saw it but only £12 was raised. By contrast 20,000 people paid a shilling a piece to see Frith's *Railway Station* in London in two weeks in 1862. Finally issued in 1864, the

fig.17 George Cruikshank Campaign Ticket for the purchase of *The Worship of Bacchus* for the Nation *c*.1863 Cliché verre engraving 11.5 × 16 Victoria & Albert Museum, London

fig.18 Pieter Breughel the Elder
(c.1525–69)
The Triumph of Death
Oil on panel
Museo Nacional del Prado,
Madrid

print too sold slowly, being of necessity too expensive for its target audience to afford, another fatal financial error. Queen Victoria saw *Bacchus*
at Windsor Castle and praised 'the design and execution',[23] but evidently
not the subject. The picture had the makings of an heroic failure and to
Cruikshank's consternation, amid acrimony the National Temperance
League finally lost patience and disowned the project, leaving the Committee of its own members to bear the monetary costs. The situation was
not rescued until 1869 when a prosperous group of temperance subscribers bought *Bacchus* and presented it to the National Gallery, Cruikshank designing a special certificate showing him sitting astride his
creation (fig.17). It never hung at Trafalgar Square, but instead at the
South Kensington Museum, later the Victoria & Albert Museum. From
1884–94 it was on loan to Bradford Art Gallery, from 1894–6 Dundee, and
from 1905–9 Newcastle. Since then, Cruikshank's great masterpiece has
been permanently in store, transferred to the Tate in 1959.

Ruskin judged Cruikshank had wasted himself in his temperance work
'in vain war with conditions of vice too low alike for record or rebuke,
among the dregs of the British populace'.[24] But *The Worship of Bacchus*
remains an important testimony to his beliefs, and the mood of the
times. It is an epic of human frailty, an exaggeration, but also a truthful

fig.19 *The Worship of Bacchus* (detail)

one. There is no pleasure in the punishment of the men being flogged and all the other incidents, only humane horror and sympathy. Cruikshank believed there was an alternative, and the picture is really about choice – to follow the temperance beacon or give in to temptation and excess. It has an unwavering moral certainty. The composition itself was perhaps partly inspired by Gillray's lampoon *Democracy, or a Sketch of the Life of Bonaparte*, a series of compartments. The crowded bodies and hierarchical arrangement of Michelangelo's *Last Judgement* must have provided a further compositional source, the tiers of sin here inverted, with the most degraded nearest their profane deity Bacchus, who replaces Christ. But a closer, previously unrecognised source is Pieter Breughel's *The Triumph of Death* (fig.18). Much copied and known through prints, Cruikshank has adopted its high horizon and network of incidents, and the hanged men, flames, and pits down to hell are found in the same position in *Bacchus*; their moralising subjects are also linked.

The riot at the picture's heart shows a society out of control, the mob has taken over, and the result is violence, murder and mayhem. This is an unregulated, uncontrolled, uncontrollable society; the police are themselves both victims and perpetrators. Cruikshank had grown up in an era horrified by the excesses of the French Revolution (in which lunatics were released, as here), and lived also through Chartist agitation, the 'Bread or Blood' riots of the post-Waterloo economic collapse, the year 1848 when half of Europe seemed in revolution, and the horror in Britain at the Indian Mutiny of 1857. Fear of the mob, of mob justice, excess and social breakdown was clearly deeply ingrained in his outlook.

But Cruikshank's picture is nevertheless a profound statement of belief in the determining factors of environment and experience in governing and moulding behaviour. It rejected the growing tendency to regard genetics and breeding as the controlling factors, as was formally postulated by the eugenicist Francis Galton in 1869. Cruikshank had long ago lampooned such standpoints by caricaturing the spurious science of phrenology, although physical type was none the less a staple of his satire. Cruikshank believed drink-led social corrosion caused inappropriate behaviour, and this was redeemable, not innate. This was a humane, humanistic viewpoint, and also a very modern one. It situated him among liberal reformers of the nineteenth and twentieth centuries who argued that better social conditions would bring not only material comfort and justice but improved civic responsibility. On one level *Bacchus* is an account of the problems of the poor, which Cruikshank, rightly or wrongly, in great part attributed to drink. On another it is an uncompromising, table-thumping, moralising sermon.

An Unexpected Postscript

Cruikshank died aged eighty-six on 1 February 1878 after suffering from bronchitis. Almost to the end he led a full and active life, and proudly attributed his physical vigour to teetotalism. Cruikshank's widow Eliza was independently well provided for, but his will contained several shocks. He left much of his estate to one Adelaide Archibold, and put capital in trust for her ten children. Living at 31 Augustus Street, a short distance from his marital home, she was evidently Cruikshank's mistress, and the children probably his too. Keeping up a second, secret house and household may explain Cruikshank's financial difficulties in later life, which even his friends could not fully account for. Drawn up in 1876, Cruikshank's will left Adelaide 'all such furniture books wines and household effects belonging to me' at the Augustus Street house. This phrase provided a further shock, for the mention of 'wines ... belonging to me' suggests Cruikshank was a secret drinker as well as effectively a bigamist. It seems so unlikely – all Cruikshank's temperance work, not least *The Worship of Bacchus*, is run through with integrity and passion. But the explicit 'belonging to me' gnaws away at our confidence. Perhaps the phrase was intended as a catch-all protection for Adelaide to ensure she kept everything funded by Cruikshank, but it still meant that alcohol was present. Whatever the truth, it provides a suitably dramatic finale to Cruikshank's long career, and a suitably satirical blast of Victorian hypocrisy.

Cruikshank on *The Worship of Bacchus*

In 1862 Cruikshank delivered a detailed lecture before *Bacchus* to temperance worthies. These brief extracts give some flavour of his oratory and ideology:

> I have not the vanity to call it a *picture*, it being merely the mapping out of certain ideas for an especial purpose, and I painted it with a view that a lecturer might use it as so many diagrams … In the centre of this mass … is a madman … It may, indeed, be said that madness prevails over the whole of this mass of worshippers; for *excitement* from strong drink and *drunkenness* is, in fact, temporary *insanity* … In the crowd … may be seen various acts of violence, cruelty, and brutality, at least as far as propriety would allow me to show them – for no artist, nor author, dare attempt to represent or describe, to the fullest extent, the horrible crimes and disgusting deeds that are committed under the influence of wine, beer, or spirits. No, it cannot, it *dare* not be done. On the left side of this mob are men and women, drinking and fighting – dreadful cruelty to children by their parents … Below this is a man beating a woman till her face is one mass of blood and bruises; this represents a scene that I witnessed in broad daylight on a Sunday afternoon – the man and the woman both under the influence of drink … under the bar is a soldier offering up his medal to Bacchus, and a woman offering up her child; a man stabbing his wife, a fellow shooting a girl; a ruffian kicking a girl in the face, a woman stabbing her husband, two thieves, primed with gin and beer, garrotting and robbing a gentleman …
>
> Although we tell where *moderation begins*, no one can tell where it may end …
>
> Here may be seen … a missionary tapping a Hindoo on the shoulder, whilst another Hindoo points to the bottle in the missionary's pocket …
>
> I believe that I have now pointed out all the various subjects … which is, after all, merely a representation of *facts* – broad, undeniable facts – the representation of which will, I hope, induce all those who have not yet adopted our principles and practices to take the matter into their most serious consideration. It is a difficult thing for a moderate drinker to understand why *he* should leave off his *small* quantity because there are others who take a *large* quantity … If they become convinced that our principles are *right*, they will at once see that by abstaining themselves they will not only help to save millions of their fellow-creatures from destruction, but will themselves, in all probability, enjoy better health and a longer life.[25]

fig.20 *The Worship of Bacchus*
(detail)

The Condition and Conservation Treatment of *The Worship of Bacchus*

Christopher Holden

The painting was in an unexhibitable condition before this display. After exhibition in London in 1863 and its subsequent provincial tour, the painting had for much of its life been exposed to smoke pollution and had been generally neglected in inadequate stores in London. Since the Clean Air Act of 1956, it is easy to forget how much smoke there was in London's air, two-thirds of which was estimated to come from house, flat and office fires (fig.21). The appearance of the painting was extremely poor, mainly due to the accumulation of a very considerable amount of dirt, which mostly consisted of soot and also to some extent the darkening of a varnish layer. These obscured much of the detail and the colours, such as they are (fig.22). There is a general network of fine age cracks in the ground and paint, with slightly elevated edges (fig.23). These are stable and are hardly visible in normal viewing conditions. In some places slightly worn areas of thinner paint indicate that a crude attempt had been made to clean the painting when it first started becoming dirty. The painting was transferred to an air-conditioned Tate store in the early 1970s, where it remained until the recent conservation treatment. Even after cleaning, the colours are rather subdued: being stored in the dark for over a hundred years has had the effect of significantly darkening the oil

fig.21 Aerial view over north London showing mainly smoke from domestic fires, 1940s
Photograph
Arnold Marsh, *Smoke: The problem of coal and the atmosphere*, Faber & Faber, 1947

fig.22 *The Worship of Bacchus*
(detail) during cleaning

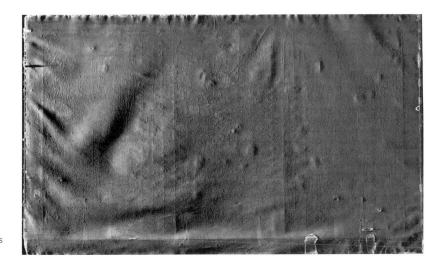

fig.23 *The Worship of Bacchus*
photographed in raking light,
showing buckling of the canvas
before conservation

medium; it has also become more transparent with ageing, which has accentuated the yellow-brown monochrome underpainting.

The linen canvas support had become fragile with age. There were fourteen accidental tears (the longest being 80 mm) and some small holes near the sides. The tacking edges had been further weakened by acidity from the supporting wooden stretcher and corrosion from the iron tacks used for the attachment. This had resulted in numerous losses and splitting of the edges in many places with the canvas literally hanging off the top edge of the stretcher by threads, and many large undulations in the canvas caused by the lack of tension (see fig.23). Pieces of the painting including the stretcher had been lost and damaged at the corners owing to careless handling in the past. The stretcher joints were distorted and the edges generally damaged. From the number of holes in the tacking edges it is clear that the painting had been removed and reattached to the stretcher at least three or four times. This is likely to have been during its tour, when the painting was rolled for transport between the different venues. A double canvas strip-lining that was stitched to the front edges of the original tacking edges, as well as tacks on the sides, would almost certainly have been added to strengthen them, probably on return to the National Gallery in 1896. There was no frame; however, evidence from near the edges of the painting show that there was one at some time, which would have included two small spandrils at the top corners.

Nearly all the dirt and discoloured varnish were removed with various solvents. The tears, damages and losses were repaired and restored and the tacking edges strengthened by the addition of synthetic canvas strips glued on the back with a specially formulated heat-seal adhesive. These

fig.24 Cross-section of paint from the upper left corner of the painting after cleaning, photographed at × 200 magnification. The width of the section shown here is 0.5mm.

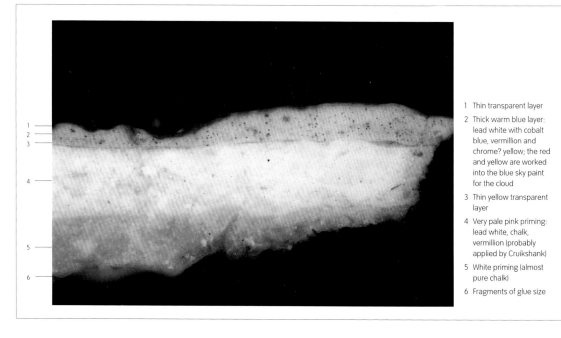

1 Thin transparent layer

2 Thick warm blue layer: lead white with cobalt blue, vermillion and chrome? yellow; the red and yellow are worked into the blue sky paint for the cloud

3 Thin yellow transparent layer

4 Very pale pink priming: lead white, chalk, vermillion (probably applied by Cruikshank)

5 White priming (almost pure chalk)

6 Fragments of glue size

were also used to attach the painting to a new stretcher, which is mainly constructed from aluminium, rather than wood, to reduce its weight and increase its rigidity. The painting was re-stretched over a loose lining canvas to give it additional overall support.

The reverse of the painting was treated with a de-acidification solution to reduce the deterioration process by neutralising the acids in it and leaving behind a buffer to absorb migrating acids from other sources. An acrylic gesso primer with a high chalk content was applied to both sides of the loose lining canvas to help stiffen it and to act as an additional buffer. The painting was re-varnished with a non-yellowing synthetic resin. There was insufficient information about the style of the earlier frame, except for the spandrils, so the new frame is based on a mid-nineteenth-century neoclassical-style moulding, partly finished with toned gilding and partly with black lacquer.

Cruikshank's Technique

Cruikshank obtained the stretcher and canvas ready made and prepared from Winsor & Newton, a well-known manufacturer and supplier of artists' materials and equipment: their stamp is still visible on the reverse of the canvas. The original wooden stretcher is made up of three separate vertical sections, joined together with removable wooden battens on the back. This would have been done so that the stretcher could be dismantled and the canvas rolled for easier transportation. The canvas is a plain-weave linen with closely woven fine threads. Microscopic examination and analysis of samples showed that Winsor & Newton had prepared the canvas with a thick glue size layer and a single priming layer of lead white and chalk bound in oil. A second priming on top of this – thin and very pale pink in colour, consisting of lead white, chalk and a small amount of vermilion – was probably applied by Cruikshank (fig.24).

Cruikshank was essentially a graphic artist and not a painter, and he did not actually paint many oils. The technique he used for this painting is very straightforward. The images have initially been drawn fairly accurately in pencil: the pencil lines are visible in many places where the paint is thin (Cruikshank had already worked out the composition and design in a smaller watercolour painting). Samples showed that over the drawing there is a thin under-painting mainly in brown and yellow-brown washes of oil paint. On top of this the images have been more clearly defined using thicker paint and colours, with brush markings in many places. The pigments that have been identified from analysis are lead white, chrome yellow, vermilion, cobalt blue, Mars brown and a reddish Mars brown. Highlights of white and tinted white impasted oil paint have been applied everywhere with vigorous squiggles, dabs and blobs and are a particular feature of the technique which gives the painting a liveliness. There is a final thin layer of natural resin varnish over the paint. A layer of dirt in between the two shows that the varnish was applied some time after the painting was finished.

Works in the Display

Dimensions are given in centimetres, height before width

Paintings, Prints and Photographs

1 George Cruikshank
The Worship of Bacchus 1860–2
Oil on canvas 236 × 406
Tate; Presented by R.E. Lofft and friends 1869

2 George Cruikshank and Charles Mottram (1807–1876)
The Worship of Bacchus 1864
Etching and engraving 64.8 × 105.1
Tate; Purchased 1978

3 George Cruikshank
The Bottle, Plate 1: The Bottle is brought out: For the First Time the Husband induces his Wife 'Just to take a Drop' 1847
Glyphograph 22 × 33
Victoria & Albert Museum, London

4 George Cruikshank
The Bottle, Plate 2: He is discharged from his Employment for Drunkenness. They pawn their Clothes to Supply the Bottle 1847
Glyphograph 22 × 33
Victoria & Albert Museum, London

5 George Cruikshank
The Bottle, Plate 3: An Execution Sweeps off the Greater Part of their Furniture. They comfort themselves with the Bottle 1847
Glyphograph 22 × 33
Victoria & Albert Museum, London

6 George Cruikshank
The Bottle, Plate 4: Unable to obtain Employment they are drawn into the Streets to Beg 1847
Glyphograph 22 × 33
Victoria & Albert Museum, London

7 George Cruikshank
The Bottle, Plate 5: Cold, Misery and Want destroy their youngest Child 1847
Glyphograph 22 × 33
Victoria & Albert Museum, London

8 George Cruikshank
The Bottle, Plate 6: Fearful Quarrels and brutal Violence are the natural consequences of the frequent use of the Bottle 1847
Glyphograph 22 × 33
Victoria & Albert Museum, London

9 George Cruikshank
The Bottle, Plate 7: The Husband kills his Wife with the Instrument of all their Misery 1847
Glyphograph 22 × 33
Victoria & Albert Museum, London

10 George Cruikshank
The Bottle, Plate 8: The bottle has done its Work – It has destroyed the Infant and the Mother, it has brought the Son and Daughter to Vice and to the Streets, and has left the Father a hopeless Maniac 1847
Glyphograph 22 × 33
Victoria & Albert Museum, London

11 George Cruikshank
The Drunkard's Children, Plate 1: Neglected by their Parents, educated only in the Streets and falling into the Hands of Wretches who live upon the Vices of others they are lead to the Gin-Shop to drink at that Fountain which nourishes every Species of Crime 1848
Glyphograph 22 × 33
Victoria & Albert Museum, London

12 George Cruikshank
The Drunkard's Children, Plate 8: The Maniac Father and Convict Brother are gone. – The Poor Girl, homeless, friendless, deserted and gin-mad, commits self-murder 1848
Glyphograph 22 × 33
Victoria & Albert Museum, London

13 George Cruikshank
The Fruits of Intemperance c.1860
Engraving 56 × 37.9
British Museum, London

14 George Cruikshank
Campaign Ticket for the purchase of *The Worship of Bacchus* for the Nation c.1867
Cliché verre etching 11.5 × 16
Victoria & Albert Museum, London

15 Robert Braithwaite Martineau (1826–69)
The Last Day in the Old Home 1862
Oil on canvas 107.3 × 144.8
Tate. Presented by E.H. Martineau 1896

16 William Hogarth (1697–1764)
Gin Lane 1751
Etching and engraving 35.7 × 30.5
Tate; Transferred from the reference collection 1973

17 Unknown photographer
George and Eliza Cruikshank c.1862
Photograph
Victoria & Albert Museum, London

Books and Pamphlets

18 George Cruikshank
The Comic Almanac 1844
Wine in a Ferment and Spirits in Hot Water
Etching 10 × 16.3
Dr Jan Piggott

19 George Cruikshank
The Comic Almanac 1838
Battle of A-gin-court
Etching 10 × 16.3
Dr Jan Piggott

20 George Cruikshank
The Comic Almanac 1842
The Parlour and the Cellar
Etching 10 × 16.3
Dr Jan Piggott

21 John Decorator Stewart, *The Worship of Bacchus, size 13 ft. 4in. by 7 ft. 8 in. painted by G. Cruikshank. The critique of the above painting by J.S. A descriptive lecture by G. Cruikshank, and opinions of the press*, London, 8th edn., 1868
National Gallery Archive

22 John B Gough, *Autobiography and Personal Recollections of John B Gough*, Springfield, Massachusetts, 1869. Illustrated by George Cruikshank; open at the plate *An Extraordinary Scene at Sadlers Wells Theatre*
Robert Upstone

Objects

23 George Cruikshank and Charles Mottram (1807–76)
Engraver's Plate for *The Worship of Bacchus* 1860–4)
Steel 68.5 × 109
The Thomas Ross Collection

24 Middlesborough Pottery
Four Tea Plates with scenes from *The Bottle* (scenes 5–8) c.1847
Printed earthenware, part enamelled, 20.7 × 20.7 × 2.2
Brighton and Hove Museums

25 Two Staffordshire Taper Holders: Ale Bench and Tee Total c.1835
Enamelled pearlware 19.9 × 18.8 × 12.6
Brighton and Hove Museums

26 Staffordshire or North East England John Gough Commemorative Cup and Saucer c.1853/c.1857
Printed earthenware 10.3 × 8.3 × 7; 14.2 × 14.2
Brighton and Hove Museums

27 Staffordshire
Tee Total Society Plate
Printed earthenware 20.7 × 20.7 × 3
Brighton and Hove Museums

28 Pirated Woodblock for *The Bottle* c.1847
Engraved wood 9 × 12.8
Jarndyce Books

Notes

1 Quoted in Robert L. Patten, *George Cruikshank's Life, Times, and Art: 1792–1835*, I, 1992, p.xxv
2 Cruikshank mss., Greater London Records Office; quoted in Hilary and Mary Evans, *The Man who Drew the Drunkard's Daughter: The Life and Art of George Cruikshank 1792–1978*, 1978, p.189
3 Quoted in Blanchard Jerrold, *The Life of George Cruikshank in Two Epochs*, 1971 edn, p.223
4 Charles Dickens, 'Gin-Shops' in *Sketches by Boz*
5 Jerrold, *Life of Cruikshank*, p.222
6 Ibid. p.254
7 Peter Quennell (ed.), *Mayhew's London: Being Selections from 'London Labour and the London Poor'*, 1969, p.66
8 See Barbara T. Gates, *Victorian Suicide: Mad Crimes and Sad Histories*, Princeton, 1988, pp.135–50
9 Eric Hobsbawm, *Industry and Empire*, 1983 edn, fig.1
10 Quoted Brian Harrison, *Drink and the Victorians*, 1971, p.26
11 Samuel Smiles, *Self Help*, 1866 rev. edn, p.3
12 Jerrold, *Life of Cruikshank*, p.257
13 ibid.
14 ibid. pp.266–7
15 *Tackling Alcohol Related Crime, Disorder, Nuisance: Action Plan*, Home Office, 2000
16 'Alcohol Problems Costing Britain £3.3 billion', Alcohol Concern press release, 11 May 2000
17 Letter to T.R. Lamont, 1 Sept. 1860; Victoria & Albert Museum Library, 86 GC Box 1; quoted in Robert L. Patten, *George Cruikshank's Life, Times, and Art: 1835–1878*, II, 1996, p.406. Frith's daughter was not so complimentary; see p.26.
18 Jerrold, *Life of Cruikshank*, p.288
19 ?Dec. 1860, Princeton MS Collection; quoted in Patten, op. cit., pp.407–8
20 Jerrold, *Life of Cruikshank*, p.294
21 *Saturday Review*, July 1863, pp.187–94
22 Jane Ellen Panton, *Leaves from a Life*, 1908, pp.101–2
23 *Art Journal*, 1863, p.128
24 *Works*, XIX, pp.76–7
25 John Decorator Stewart, *The Worship of Bacchus, size 13 ft. 4in. by 7 ft. 8 in. painted by G. Cruikshank. The critique of the above painting by J.S. A descriptive lecture by G. Cruikshank, and opinions of the Press*, 1868, pp.8–17

Photographic Credits

Brighton and Hove Museums/Stella Bedoe 9

British Museum 16

Museo Nacional del Prado, Madrid 18

Dr Jan Piggott 6

Tate Photography 1, 2, 3, 4, 11, 12, 13, 14, 19, 20, 22, 23, 24

V&A Picture Library 5, 7, 8, 10, 15, 17

Index